A VENDOR'S GUIDE TO SUCCESS

HOW TO GO FROM
$0-$100K

CECILIA J. PENN-DIALLO

A Vendors Guide To Success : How to Go From $0-$100K

Copyright © 2021 by Cecilia Penn-Diallo

All rights reserved. No part of this book may be used or reproduced in any manner whatsoever without written permission except in the case of brief quotations embodied in critical articles or reviews.

First Edition: August 2021

Unless otherwise noted, all scripture references are from the King James Version of the Bible.

ISBN: 978-1-7375508-0-8
For more information contact:
Name : Cecilia Penn-Diallo
Email : thevendorcoach@gmail.com

Book Cover Design by Success Geeks Inc.
Printed in the United States of America

Dedication

I want to first thank God for giving me the strength and fortitude to do all that I have done over the years, especially within the last three years. This book is dedicated to my grandmother, Joan Savoy Penn, whom I received inspiration from. Thank you for showing me the way. My grandmother started the Jewels By Joan business in the early 1990s. She grew this business, and when she passed, I decided to keep her legacy alive by taking it over.

I would also like to dedicate this book to my husband, Saliou Diallo, and my son, Bachir Diallo, who has supported me from day one. They have given me the space to expand my business and have supported me since day one. For this, I am extremely grateful. And to my mother, Mary Penn-Beveney, who consistently supports me and covers me in prayer. To my mentor, Rochelle Wilson, who pushed me outside of the box to finally write this book (despite my hesitancy), I am extremely grateful and thank God for you in my life.

To the original Jewels By Joan 2 staff, (my rock) sister LaVida, Tonya, Tracy, Joy, JaNell, Kiera, and Diaka. To my close family and friends who have been my tribe and my help whenever I call on them. My team over the years has carried me and been my backbone. You guys have stretched and grown with me, and I am so very appreciative. And to all my customers, without you, there would be no Jewels By Joan 2. You all have rocked with me for years.

Table of Contents

Introduction   1

Chapter 1: The Story   5

Chapter 2: Getting Started   11

Chapter 3: Be True to Your Brand   27

Chapter 4: Customer Service   39

Chapter 5: The Power of Your Unique Factor   59

Chapter 6: The Setup   67

Chapter 7: Lessons Learned   89

About the Author   115

Introduction

This book came about after starting my business The Vendor Coach, a network and safe space for people in the beginning stages of their businesses. Whether it is in the vending space or not, the goal is to help them launch and start their businesses, no matter how small the business may be. When I started The Vendor Coach, I discovered that people really need easily accessible resources and assistance just to launch the businesses they wanted to start. This is what I want the book to accomplish. Many people don't feel confident about starting a business, which is unfortunate, but it is also understandable since people also lack the skills to do so. If you consider yourself in this class, I want you to know that I wrote this book just for you because I know what it's like to question and or doubt yourself and whether you should be in business. It is my hope that this book encourages you and teaches you exactly what you need to get started. You will walk away from this book with an "I can do this" mentality to launch the business.

A Vendor's Guide to Success: How to Go from $0–$100k

You may have begun reading this book unsure, but you will be ready to start your business by the time you finish. Starting is the biggest hurdle for most business owners. As a business coach for vendors, the one barrier I see in many of my clients is the drive to start. I will show you in this book how you can leverage your passion as the beginning point of starting or expanding your business.

This book will be a quick reference filled with proven strategies for success. It is my desire to share my experiences to help other small business owners. I want business owners to be able to use this as a resource that they can carry around with them, keep on the nightstand, and refer back to anytime during your journey to help motivate you and jumpstart your business. While the road has not been easy for me, it has been rewarding. I want to use my story to help encourage those beginning their journey in the vending world as well as those who are business owners. By the end of this book, you will not only be inspired to start your business, but you will have solid tools and proven strategies to help you launch or grow successfully.

Most people talk themselves out of success, and I want you to stop self-sabotaging yourself. You must believe in yourself. I don't care what people say or think.

If God told you to start the business and you believe God, then start the business. Never in a million years did I see myself writing this book. But because of my experiences, I can now share what I have learned with the world.

Introduction

Once I stepped into being my authentic self, I moved. I also tapped into my network, my tribe, my family. They have always pushed and supported me. I have been successful not because I am perfect or the best in the industry but because I started believing in myself. I didn't let people tear down my dream. I got away from people who spoke negativity into my space while speaking ill of me and my business.

As you embark on your journey as a business owner, always remember to keep your goal in front of you, walk in faith, push, stand on your purpose, and exhibit fortitude. If you lack any of these things, seek God and he will give you what you need. Keep God in the equation always because he will give you the fortitude for the long haul. You must understand that being in business is not for the faint at heart. It is not for the short term, one and down, but it is for the long haul. So as you read this book, I want to encourage you to never give up, believe in yourself, and love what you do no matter what you face.

CHAPTER 1

The Story

It all started when I was about twelve years old when I would go to vending shows with my grandmother. She was the Original Queen of Bling Bling! She developed a reputation for selling unique high-fashion jewelry that was out of sight. My grandmother would allow me to help her set up and work at various vending shows. She sold Sarah Coventry Jewelry and eventually branched out into her own line of high-fashion jewelry, clothing, and accessories. She was always in fashion. I remember the days when we would pack my grandmother's Lincoln Town car to the brim. She sold everything! I would be so mad because she had so much stuff it was hard to keep track of it all. In high school, I did a lot of vending with my grandmother, and because of that, it made me grow up and mature faster.

It now has all come full circle and makes perfect sense because I do the same thing. I didn't know then that I was picking up things from her—little things like not sitting drinking cups on our table, keeping the display table free

A Vendor's Guide to Success: How to Go from $0–$100k

from clutter so customers can see all the products, providing outstanding customer service, etc. I now exhibit many of these qualities as a businesswoman. My grandmother taught me the importance of excellent customer service, which I honor until this day. She taught me that my customer is my number one priority and that I must do all things in excellence. From bagging and packaging to how we speak to our customers, it is all important. Although I earned an MBA in 2020 and have a Bachelor's in Business Administration, the lessons I learned from my grandmother cannot be matched to any concept I have learned in school.

My grandmother passed away in 2005 and a few years later in 2008 I picked up the business strong with encouragement from my family and friends. I needed the extra money, and I knew this would be a good way to honor my grandmother's legacy. When I decided to move forward, I added the "2" to the business name Jewels By Joan (2). This allowed me to carry my grandmother with me everywhere I went. Her likeness is on our banners and all other marketing materials. She was one of my biggest influences. She kept me looking good, on my toes, never settling and always wanting more. My grandmother didn't play and always made sure she looked good before leaving the house. I called her prim and proper because her standards were high. I miss my grandmother so much. I wish she could see me, the business, and how we have grown to date. She

The Story

would be amazed. I even wish she could see how we have grown tremendously during a pandemic and have been so successful with Instagram Lives. **I know she would be smiling from ear to ear, knowing that I now have my own collection, The Cecilia J Collection, which will launch very soon.**

People can sometimes be fooled by the success of someone's business. They see my progression and success over the years but don't know the blood, sweat, and tears invested. In 2017, I was struggling financially even though I was working full time, earning six figures. My problem was self-discipline and money management. As a result of poor decisions, I faced a very tough dilemma—filing bankruptcy. Yep, you heard it right. Your girl had to file bankruptcy. Most people don't understand that being in business takes so much hard work, and it is typically not as easy as it seems. When I filed for bankruptcy, I was working and selling jewelry. I had to close Jewels by Joan 2 and dissolve the business as a part of the bankruptcy, which hurt me to my core. How could I have let this happen? What would my grandmother think of me? Part of me questioned my decision. I didn't want to face the embarrassment, and I knew the stigma that comes with filing bankruptcy. I also had a huge tax bill that haunted me like a horror movie. By the time I sorted out everything, I had lost my luxury car, and my bank account was on zero, even negative.

A Vendor's Guide to Success: How to Go from $0–$100k

I wanted to share this in the beginning because most people don't realize where I have been and think things have always been great. After my financial setback, I had to work very hard in both my job and my business. Things got better; with lots of hard work and a totally different mindset, I got out of debt. Not only did I get out of debt, but I also have solid savings and a car that is paid in full. Don't tell me what God can't do! I pray that something from this book will inspire you and help you grow your business in ways you could have only dreamed of.

The Story

Capture any thoughts and comments you have after reading this chapter. How will this chapter help you?

CHAPTER 2

Getting Started

OK! Let's Go! Before you start making anything or finalizing your brand, go and see what is currently being offered in the marketplace. See how you can match your gifts and talents to show something unique and different to the marketplace. Do your research! Go to different shows and look at what is available, both in your industry and outside your industry. Take a note of what you see that aligns with your vision as a business owner. After you have finalized your concept, gather a few friends and family members and share your concept with them. The important part of this process is to get feedback from them. Let them try your product, eat it, or test it. I have used my family for years to help me with business concepts. I am grateful for them because they have always supported me and given honest feedback.

You also need a plan to advertise and market your business. Social media has become a way of life. Some business owners are afraid of it, but unfortunately, you must be

A Vendor's Guide to Success: How to Go from $0–$100k

present on social media if you want to be in business nowadays. Share flyers on social media, and have postcards ready if necessary. You can also post flyers and business cards on bulletin boards to help improve your business exposure. Marketing is so critical for every business owner and can be very expensive. I always suggest using all the free marketing resources available, starting with social media before spending money.

Let's look at some quick steps that will help you get your business off the ground.

Start your business by following these eight easy steps:

1. Pick your niche and target market.

2. Study the competition.

3. Develop a **business** plan.

4. Choose a creative name (with an available domain).

5. Design a product line.

6. Choose whether to outsource manufacturing and suppliers or not if handcrafted.

7. Devise a unique brand aesthetic—what sets you apart.

8. Develop a marketing strategy.

Getting Started

Most importantly, in all that you will ever do as an entrepreneur from the time you start until you expand, don't give up. We can talk strategy all day, but you must have the endurance to push each day, as giving up is never an option. You must believe in yourself, trust God, and keep pushing.

Whenever your business isn't going so well, pull on your tribe and your network. Ask your tribe to support you by sharing your business with their networks. This kind of connection will go a long way. I want to share some areas that you will need to consider as you are starting your business.

Start-Up Basics: What You Need to Know

Make Things Legal

It's best to make things legal before you start selling services or products. Some businesses don't need heavy legal or business registration before starting, but checking these boxes first is advised. You can do this by registering it as a proprietorship or limited liability company if you want to keep your personal and business assets separate from each other.

If you're not sure which direction to go in, you can check with your local authorities. They can tell you what licenses you need to get your business up and running.

A Vendor's Guide to Success: How to Go from $0–$100k

Create a Website

You won't be able to sell products if you don't market yourself and have an avenue through which people can purchase. This is where your website comes in. You've got a couple of options here. You could go with free websites through WIX and Go Daddy. They do offer platforms to do e-commerce.

You can also use Shopify, which is a good option for selling products. If you don't want to build the site yourself, you can always hire someone to build it for you. These days, sites are a lot easier to build with so many small business owners helping startups create budget-friendly websites.

Promote Your Product

Setting up an online store to sell your products is simple and inexpensive.

- Post your product for sale online and on your website.

- Use Facebook and Instagram Ads.

- Promote in various Facebook Groups.

- Post! Even if only one person likes your post, keep posting!

Getting Started

Find Your Why

From experience, your mindset is everything. Take the time to reset your attitude and get clarity on why you are in business. Losing it all is very hard, even devastating, but lingering around with a loser's attitude makes everything even harder. Being clear on your "why" will give you fortitude and stamina. When things get tough, don't lose hope. No pity parties! Use your why as your motivation to rebuild. Do this by developing your company's mission and vision statement

Network Like Crazy

Learn who's in your tribe. Identify your values and have a list of questions to determine if someone shares your vision. Spend as much time as you can attending as many events as possible to meet a diverse group of people who can promote your business.

Being unique enough to stand out online and in person is **everything**. At the same time, it's ridiculously hard, but keep at it. Every business constantly evolves and changes—don't worry; just keep pushing!

Decide on Your Pricing

Once you have established the foundational pieces of your business, you can decide on your pricing. This involves identifying the customer rates, whether you are selling products or goods or providing a service. If you are not

A Vendor's Guide to Success: How to Go from $0–$100k

sure about the price point you should be setting, you can look at similar businesses and often your competitors. You can get that competitive advantage if you price a little under your competition. Look at what other industries are charging and establish your price point accordingly. You can shift your prices up and down depending on your "at cost" rate.

Start-up costs can vary depending on your industry and type of business. As always, upfront research is a must. Research will give you the knowledge and understanding needed to make the most informed decisions. If you are selling jewelry and accessories, you can give yourself some flexibility because there are so many options. Essentially, you can start based on what you have the budget for.

For example, you may say, "I have $300 allocated to buy jewelry." You can resell that jewelry and get a return on your investment as long as you don't buy too high. If you buy too high, then you may just break even. In this scenario, you want a quick return on your investment so you can buy more inventory. Ideally, you want to buy low with the potential to increase the price of your product. The rule of thumb in retail is 2.5% on top of the cost of goods. But this can vary greatly depending on location, demographics, and products. If you are into crafts or making things like candles or anything crafty, the amount would depend on the cost of supplies needed to make the items.

Getting Started

If you make shea butter, you will need to factor in all the butter, oils, jars, labels, perfumes, etc. that goes with making and packaging your shea butter. Research different options so that you get the most economically feasible option. You may have to purchase from local vendors for your supplies before you go with big-time manufacturers.

I started my business with $500, and the rest is history. It was all I had and could afford at that time, so it became my budget, just that easy. I knew it would give me a good head start with a particular wholesaler that I knew from my grandmother. I purchased jewelry from that vendor and just continued to invest after the business started to gain speed. I have used this process over the years and have seen JBJ2 prosper and expand. You may have to do this type of budgeting for a while even when you start to make a couple of thousand dollars because this will help you grow. You will need to use those funds to keep inventory on hand, especially if you are shipping products. If you need heavy equipment and machinery to start your business like a restaurant or print company, the start-up costs will be more. If you are selling jewelry, accessories, candles, or even providing a service, your start-up costs can be minimal. Many people think you need thousands of dollars to start a business. Not so! Not all industries require large capital to start, so decide wisely.

Take advantage of low-cost options to start marketing materials like Adobe Spark, Canva, and Pic Collage. So

A Vendor's Guide to Success: How to Go from $0–$100k

much is available to help you capture your products and promote your business, and it is all free. One of my mentees uses Canva for logos, flyers, and designs. She started her business with little to no money and has been able to get what she needs to sell and re-invest back into her business. If you must start your business on a budget, you have options. Canva is a big one for logo creation, and Adobe Spark is good for flyers and social media templates.

If you take away nothing else from this chapter, take away this—Consistency, Consistency, Consistency! You don't need a lot of money, followers, etc., but you do need Consistency! Without that, you will fail. You must be consistent in promoting your brand, posting on social media, and engaging the people who follow you. You can't be in business one day a week. Do you want to make money one day a week? No, you always have to engage and continue to build business. You do this with consistently engaging with your customers. Constantly ask people to share your page. Establish that you are a legit business and not just here for the moment. I consistently invested back into my business. Although I got a jump start because of my grandmother's wholesaler connections, I still consistently invested back into my business. I consistently look for new vendors and relationships to build. I consistently take a temperature check of the brand and see what needs to be changed. I consistently engage on social media with all my followers, from funny pics to business quotes to current events.

Getting Started

The "Do's" of Getting Started

Starting a business is very much like running a race: Preparation and practice are keys to success. Now, let me just share some tips that will help you enter the entrepreneurial race with drive and passion as you are pursuing your dreams.

First, you must go into this knowing that your competition will always make a quick dash to the finish line.

I don't want you to get distracted as you are climbing. Go at your own pace and never take yourself out of the race because of what you see other people doing. Don't let doubt kick in. You must believe in yourself and your product and stand by your brand. Even through the tough times and hurdles, you must stay in the race. You'll see your business grow and blossom right before your eyes. I call the following tips the "Do's" of starting up! My hope is that they will help you in your journey and help you overcome and survive the hurdles that entrepreneurs may face on the road to startup and expansion.

1. **DO "Have a Positive Attitude":** You must think positive all the time. Think of the positive outcomes only and find a way to stay focused. Stay away from negative people, thoughts, and self-doubt about your capacity. Surround yourself with people who believe in you and support you because negativity can dampen your enthusiasm and passion. Stay away from negative

A Vendor's Guide to Success: How to Go from $0–$100k

people (even family) and those who are waiting for you to fail. All of this can be very emotionally and mentally draining. And don't fall prey to procrastination and self-sabotage, which can come because of negative people, negative thoughts, and self-doubt. DO believe in yourself at every moment!

1. **DO "Refresh" Your Connections:** Your goal is to connect with people who want to support your business and are willing to help you if things get difficult. Connect with people who are in similar stages in their business and are also trying to grow. Join professional organizations and seek out successful business owners you want to model. Locate organizations in your own community where other entrepreneurs get together and support each other. These affiliations can lead to advice and networking connections and are a great source for potential clients.

2. **DO "Shore Up" Your Future:** Assess and always work to eliminate risks. Risks can only become surprises if you avoid critical information up front. So do all the legwork required to shore up your plans ahead of time. As you create your plans, consider both your short-term and long-term goals. Think about your business growth and all the ramifications of your need for cash or talent to help you grow.

Getting Started

3. **DO "Exhaust" Your Creativity:** Think creatively about how you'll get your products in front of people. Think about creative ways you can get visibility. Get some inspiration by reading about different companies and how they've succeeded and learned about the practices that differentiate them from others. Keep thinking about new ways to do things that will allow your business to stand out.

4. **DO "Support" Your Credentials:** Work with business coaches and mentors to add to your knowledge and skill set. You might have a great idea and may be really skilled in an area, but you may have a few weak spots. Investigate local organizations to see if they offer business classes and workshops designed to help you supplement your credentials in different business-related areas like marketing, budgeting, funding, technology, operations, and financial management.

5. **DO "Polish" Ideas:** A great way to refine your ideas and really hash them out is to write them down in a place where you can find them at any given moment. I always say that you need a few journals in different places to write down things. There's no time like the present to start your "business journal." This can either be in the form of a traditional spiral-bound notebook or something fancy. Various tools can help you keep track of important notes and your ideas.

A Vendor's Guide to Success: How to Go from $0–$100k

These ideas can eventually be rolled up into your business plan, which will become the road map for your business.

6. **DO "Reframe" Your Perspective:** As you begin writing down your thoughts and ideas, don't give up just because you may have to make some adjustments. This is normal and has likely happened to all of us. As a future successful entrepreneur or an expanding one, you can't afford to become fixed on any one way of doing things. Make sure factors influencing your decisions include the environment, technology, your budget, and your time. All these things are always shifting, and you might have to tweak your ideas to make them work. Even if you have to tweak, tweak! Just don't give up!

7. **DO "Realign" Your Hopes & Dreams:** Clarifying what you really want to do as an entrepreneur is the key to your future success. If you don't know what you love to do, then your dreams should remain just dreams. Successful people tend to do what they love. Dreaming about owning your own business but not exploring who you are and what you love won't help you move closer to the reality of successful entrepreneurship. You must explore and research what is needed to materialize those dreams. You must do this to identify whether it aligns with your desired outcome.

Getting Started

8. **DO "Document" Your Growth & Performance:** Keeping track of your successes and milestones is critical to your overall success. So set goals for yourself and your business and chart your progress. Revisit your plans to make sure you're on target. If you're not, evaluate why and make corrections to get back on track. You can use your results later to sell clients on why they should support your business. Many business owners forget the importance of setting goals and modifying those goals based on real-life performance.

9. **DO "Map-Out" What's Next:** People who write goals and plans are much more likely to achieve them than people who just visualize success. They have a much better chance of actually being successful. The success of your business depends on preparation, practice, and planning. Create a vision for what your business should look like and create a blueprint to get there. The great thing about the blueprint is that it gives you direction as you start the journey and keeps you focused while you are in the trenches.

It's Hard Work

Even though I saw how my grandmother worked so hard, I wish she were here to tell me how much work this would be. Maintaining and growing a business is hard work, from managing social media to refreshing your logos and digital

A Vendor's Guide to Success: How to Go from $0–$100k

collateral. It is hard work! Securing graphic and web designers that align with your brand is challenging. Managing your customers is key and will intensify over the years. People will not want to buy from you if you don't respond to their needs.

Then, there is the whole back-end side of your business, including order fulfillment, taxes, staff, and branding. If you are an entrepreneur, then you should be paying taxes. It is your responsibility. Do not get into entrepreneurship and think you will get a big return every year. You can't keep writing off losses so that you can get a return. What do you do when you go from mailing three to five packages a week to 200-plus packages a week? It is a great problem to have, but it can be taxing. Every business owner needs to plan for growth, and you plan for growth before you grow. If you don't, then your own business growth will overwhelm you. I am not complaining about where I am, but I just wish someone would have nudged me. It would not have changed my mind about going into business, but I would have been a little more prepared.

Take one step at a time, one action at time; believe God and be consistent. If you put God in front of your business, he will lead the way and help you along your journey.

Getting Started

Capture any thoughts and comments you have after reading this chapter. How will this chapter help you?

CHAPTER 3

Be True to Your Brand

Being true to your brand can lead to business success. Whether you are a new business owner or have been operating your company for years, you know how important it is to get the message out about your product or service. **Be true to your brand!**

Make sure all your digital and visual imagery, such as your website, looks, feels, and reads in a way that conveys your brand, your benefits, your unique factor. If you want people to take note, you must prove to them that you are noteworthy. If you want people to begin identifying with you and your brand, you must be consistent.

I've seen great business owners who are incredibly personable and fun to be around, with super boring websites that just do not do them justice. On the other hand, I've seen very serious brands with loud or fun websites or

A Vendor's Guide to Success: How to Go from $0–$100k

marketing that simply does not represent them properly. If you are fun... show it! If you are serious... show it! Whatever your brand is...whatever your message is, make sure you continue to be consistent and clear in all your marketing. **Don't worry about people saying that you are doing too much! Shout out your message!**

These tips have helped me build an ever-increasing client base and grow my brand with many levels of success.

Be consistent—Customers know when there is a disconnect between what you have promised and what they receive. To be successful, businesses need to be consistent, offering their customers the same values, honesty, and quality products and services each time. Be authentic—Image is truly worth a thousand words. As a business, never claim to be something you are not. Stay authentic to yourself and your core values. Customers will love you for being your true, authentic self. My customers know I cannot pronounce words correctly. It is what it is! I am not perfect. But we laugh and joke about it, and they always help me on my Lives to try and pronounce words correctly. It's a running joke, but that is being authentic to me, and they love me for it! You must understand your customers and what your product or service brings to their community. Everything your business does should be a representation of you and the message you are trying to convey.

Understand customers—Think about your customers daily and try to understand that what your company

28

Be True to Your Brand

does has an impact on customers. Things such as pricing, new products, or even new messaging must always consider their needs and feedback. Put yourself consistently in their shoes to find out how they see your business. Understand what your product means to your customers and their sense of identity.

Stay competitive—To thrive, you must stay relevant and competitive. Staying true to your brand does not mean refusing to evolve but being willing to be aware.

You must be aware of what's happening and what is changing in your industry. You must regularly monitor what is new in the industry and be in tune with your customers' ever-changing needs.

Reach Out—Invite customers to be part of the company's launch and growth through feedback or surveys. Social media makes it easier for customers to participate in your business's efforts using online photos, reviews, or uplifting stories.

Be a walking advertisement—Do you use your own product or service? If the answer is no, there is a huge problem. Stop right here and reread the introduction and chapter one! If you do, continue reading. You should be your first brand ambassador, and if that is not happening, you may want to reconsider why you are in business. Every business owner should use their own product, wear it, and consume it.

29

A Vendor's Guide to Success: How to Go from $0–$100k

Below, I have outlined some simple steps to help you create a successful brand and brand identity. These steps have helped me grow JBJ2 to where it is right now and why I am able to write this book.

STEP 1: DO YOUR RESEARCH

Whether you are starting a new company or expanding, research should be your first step. The more knowledge you can gain about your industry, the better. Research will also help you find your competitors and potential competitors. Doing the proper research can help you understand the dos and don'ts of your industry. You will find what works for certain companies and what does not work.

STEP 2: CREATE YOUR MISSION AND VISION STATEMENT

Mission and vision statements make up the foundation of your business. It's crucial to understand the difference and remain true to both statements. Your mission statement summarizes your company's values and should be your company's reason for existing. It has a direct effect on your brand identity. You must take the time and effort to create a statement that your company truly believes.

Your vision statement is your company desired future position. What do you want to see your company do long-term? The work you do every day will eventually get you to "that place." Vision statements are about looking ahead

30

Be True to Your Brand

and focusing on goals to reach. Use your vision statement as a guide for your company in the coming years.

SAMPLE

The Vendor Coach Mission and Vision Statement

My Mission

To help emerging small businesses and event/conference planners maximize efforts in the area of on-site vending opportunities and product development. Provide expert advise to conference and event planners for the development and maximization of successful results through vending and vendor management.

My Vision

To empower and inspire business owners to maximize their potential.

STEP 3: DESIGN

In researching and preparing to write this book, I discovered that only 7% of communication is verbal. That means that 93% of what you communicate about your company's brand image is nonverbal and this is where design comes in. Your customer will visit your website, social media, or store and immediately form an opinion about your company based on the aesthetics.

31

A Vendor's Guide to Success: How to Go from $0–$100k

Design a logo that your customers will learn to recognize. Your logo is one of the best ways to create an initial connection with your customer. Think about your brand's colors, as different colors can have a huge impact on potential customers. Choose a color palette that reflects your company's values and voice. Your website will be your best brand ambassador, so make sure it is designed well. Investing in your website design will pay off in the long run. Make sure it is easy to navigate and the content is broken down into small sections for readers to easily digest. Take time to organize your content in a way that will make sense to visitors and create the best experience. Make sure customers can easily pay for their items.

STEP 4: YOUR STAFF/TEAM

Your brand image can reach as far as your team takes it. Please choose your team wisely.

Hiring people with values that match your company's values will affect your customers positively. You don't want to hire just willing workers. Hire people who connect with your vision.

During the interviewing process, be sure to ask the right questions to understand who the interviewee is and what matters to them. Give them scenarios that align with how your business flows. Your brand (even if your personal brand is you!) is your promise to your customers. It's what you stand for and what makes you unique.

Be True to Your Brand

And your team helps you sustain that. You can't afford to have team members who compromise your mission and values. You want your customers to know your brand. You want a consistent reputation. You want to build longevity, and your team plays a critical role in ensuring that this happens.

Adapt and Remain Flexible

Adapting does not necessarily mean changing your beliefs and values. It means keeping up with the times as it relates to your industry. Changes don't mean you throw your business plan out the window and start something new. It just means you may have to adapt and shift some things around. New competitors arrive and expectations change. Be flexible in allowing your vision and strategy to change. As a business owner, being able to adapt to various market shifts or demand is key. If you don't, you could become stuck and outdated.

For instance, when I first launched, The Cecilia J Collection was not my original name. It was "CeCe Fashion House," which I absolutely loved. When I went to trademark the name, the name was taken. This was devastating. I could not imagine another name. I felt stuck, like I could not move forward. I quickly realized though that I had to move forward. Would I let something small as a name stop my *dream?* Heck No! It was not easy, but I did move forward. I mourned the loss of my original name

A Vendor's Guide to Success: How to Go from $0–$100k

and quickly pivoted to researching and using my creative brain process to discover a new name. I stayed up for about two nights straight trying to decide the new name. I spoke with family and friends just to talk things through. I wanted a new name that would represent me, my brand, and my story. I was excited when I finally decided on the name "The Cecilia J Collection." Cecilia, of course, is my name, and J stands for Joan, which is my middle name and my grandmother's name. I was excited and ready to move forward. As business owners, things will *always* come up! It's ok; take one thing at a time! What's important is how you remain flexible, pivot, and adapt to situations that come your way.

Confidence in Brand Strategy

Identifying a brand strategy will help you stay on course and remain consistent, which allows you to feel confident in your brand—even when you feel your customers are going off course. You must document how, what, where, when, and to whom you plan to communicate your brand. And when the time comes to shift that brand strategy, you will already be prepared because you have a plan. This will put you in a better position to do so.

Your brand will evolve over and over, and that doesn't mean that you lose your brand. You just adjust your brand strategy accordingly. That way, you still know who you are and what you want your business to become. Your brand

Be True to Your Brand

strategy should identify ways to capture what customers think. While you won't be everything to everyone, you must be clear about your brand. Know your customer base and who you want to be.

So, let's chat about your brand. Have you clearly identified your brand and personality? Have you determined how your brand presents itself?

Have you defined a target audience? Have you defined what sets your business apart? If not, do it! You will be doing yourself a huge favor and giving your business a more solid foundation. Marketing something that is clearly defined and organized is so much easier. *Knowing* who you are will relieve unnecessary strain on your business, and it will become a piece of cake to market yourself. A well-defined brand is an advantage for any business.

If you haven't figured this out and need help with branding, find a professional branding expert to help you strategize. Look for someone who has a proven track record and success with their own business or the business of others.

You can use social media to find some awesome branding and marketing professionals. No matter your brand strategy, if you take nothing else from this book... get this....

A Vendor's Guide to Success: How to Go from $0–$100k

You will irritate people, there will be haters, you will scare people off, and you will rub people the wrong way if you are doing it right. Don't try to make everyone happy. Just focus on making your ideal customers happy. Let your personality shine through, and make sure everything you put out conveys that message. **Be true to your brand, yourself and your customer.**

Be True to Your Brand

Capture any thoughts and comments you have after reading this chapter. How will this chapter help you?

CHAPTER 4

Customer Service

Customer service is and should be the foundation of any business. Whether you have a storefront business, online business, or are a vendor, customer service must be a priority. I truly believe my biggest success point is customer service. My grandmother taught me well! She worked extremely hard, ensuring that her customers were happy and satisfied. Many people say I have so much patience with customers, and it comes from her. My grandmother would tell her customers that she didn't have an issue with rectifying a problem or issuing a refund. When you hear me say "okay, love, I will take care of that," that is how my grandmother handled her customers. I now see how all she was doing played an important role in her ability to retain customers. As a business owner, your biggest goal must be customer retention.

You don't just want "one and done" customers but repeat customers. Your goal must be to have customers who continue to purchase from you no matter what. Your

A Vendor's Guide to Success: How to Go from $0–$100k

level of customer service will dictate your clients' loyalty level. When customers feel like you will go all out to make sure they are happy, they will ride with you. These types of ride-or-die customers will buy your stuff even if other people are selling it. Over the years, I have grown my customer base because of this approach. Don't get me wrong; I also have bad experiences with customers because people can take you to the edge and take advantage of your kindness. However, I use the same approach with all my customers, and it helps me manage them. I love my customers because many of them are so loyal. I sell many different products to different types of women and men, and my approach is the same. Whether you are a lawyer, doctor, or single mother, I will give you excellent customer service. If you spend $5 or $500 with me, I treat all my customers the same.

It's very important to invest in quality products that you can stand by. And if there is a breach or something is wrong, own and take care of your customers. Selling poor-quality products can run them away.

To maintain customers, you will need to have a positive attitude toward them most of the time. Now, we all have bad days, but as a business owner, every day can't be bad, or you might just be putting yourself out of business.

Many entrepreneurs treat customers as if they are just a number; I don't! I make it personal and focus on making connections. One way to make that connection is

Customer Service

not being so formal. Don't get me wrong; there is a time and a place for all of the formal stuff; however, don't let your formal presentation turn them off. An overly formal presentation can build a wall and give your customer the impression that they cannot connect with you. Having a more informal tone with your customers could also help minimize conflict. And this is not just for business owners with stores or those who do a lot of showcasing at events and shows; this is also for those who engage with customers online.

People can get very confrontational if they feel they are not being treated well. Being formal can sometimes add fuel to the fire. You will encounter confrontational customers, and it may lead to conflict. It is important to know that the conflict could arise even if you didn't do anything wrong. This is why it is so important to have the right presentation. I am always positive with my customers, and I use very positive language when engaging and interacting with them. Incorporating positive language into your presentation will not only help you avoid conflict but also prevent conflict with customers. Positive language is a great way to avoid what I call "out of the blue" conflicts.

You can also shift your words and Use positive language to redirect conversations that can turn into conflict. Redirecting customer conversations from negative to positive makes them feel they are a priority and decreases the likelihood of conflict materializing. And customers will

41

begin to trust you more because they can positively engage with you. Customer appreciation is another retention strategy that I use. In 2020, I had a customer appreciation event. It was free and was my way of saying thank you to my loyal customers. Some of my customers traveled many miles to attend. I even invited the ladies who helped me at the post office to attend the event because I truly appreciate them for making sure that I get many packages out every week

Customer Service Tips

What is the most important thing you can do to reduce customer issues and increase customer referrals? The answer is often overlooked: improve your customer service.

No matter how amazing you think your product is or how fantastic you think your team is, what matters to your customers most is their direct contact with you, your team, and your brand. Your customer service and customer relationships matter. If customers are not handled properly, your customer relationships will deteriorate, and your business growth will be negatively impacted. I take pride in my ability to build strong relationships with my customers. I want to share some tips that you can use and share with your team members.

Customer Service

Tips to Support Quality Customer Service

1. Practice Consistency, Practice Patience, Practice Empathy

2. Know Good Customer Service is an Ongoing Process

3. Ask Customers if They Understand

4. Show Your Customers Your Work Ethic

5. Don't Be Afraid to Say "I Don't Know"

6. Have Thick Skin

7. Pay Attention to Your Customer's Experience

8. Show Your Customers You're Human

9. Listen Carefully

10. Admit Your Mistakes

11. Follow Up After a Problem is Resolved

12. Get Personal

13. Be Accessible

14. Give the VIP Treatment

15. Create a Customer Network

16. Collect Customer Feedback in a Customer Friendly Way

A Vendor's Guide to Success: How to Go from $0–$100k

17. Know Your Customers

18. Communicate Clearly and Concisely

19. Don't Be Rude and Stiff

20. Don't Use Negative Language

21. Always Use Positive Language

22. Solve Problems Quickly

23. Close Conversations Correctly

24. Surprise Customers with a Thank You and Appreciation

25. Remember that Customer Service is Everyone's Job

Here's the breakdown of the aforementioned and all of which has helped JBJ2 grow and earn over 100k in the midst of a national pandemic.

Practice Consistency, Practice Empathy, and Practice Patience

Many of your customers will have questions off and on, some will want to just chat, and others will just be challenging. In all instances, you must be prepared to empathize with your customers and provide excellent service every time.

Customer Service

Know That Good Customer Service Is an Ongoing Process

Every customer service situation is different. To handle all types of scenarios and surprises, address new challenges accordingly and be willing to keep learning. Strive to have a deep understanding of your customer's needs and challenges and continue to search for better ways to address them.

Ask Customers if They Understand

Make sure your customers know what you are communicating and what you always mean. You don't want your customers to think they are getting 50% off when you really mean buy one get one 50% off. Ask customers if they understand what you're communicating.

Use positive language, stay positive, and never end a conversation without confirming the customer understands.

Show Your Customers Your Work Ethic

Customers appreciate supporting businesses whose owners work hard to provide quality experiences and products. You must stay focused on your goals to achieve the right balance so that your customers feel like you are worth supporting.

Don't Be Afraid to Say "I Don't Know"

Customers rely on you to know your product inside out. It's your job to stay informed and be ready to respond to questions. If you don't know the answer, it is okay to say

A Vendor's Guide to Success: How to Go from $0–$100k

to your customers, "I don't know, let me get back to you," as long as you follow it up with "but I'll find out." Your customers will appreciate your honesty and your willingness to get them the information they need.

You Have to Have Thick Skin

There's a lot of truth to the saying "the customer's always right." The best customer service person can swallow pride and accept blame and/or negative feedback. You will have to exhibit the capacity to handle unreasonable customers in an empathetic way. Yes! Those customers who are confrontational for no reason. No matter what, your customer's happiness is your primary goal. If a customer is completely unreasonable, just be authentic with them and maintain a level head. Let them know that you are doing your best.

Pay Attention to Your Customer's Experience

Negative customer experiences can destroy your customer relationships. Please pay close attention to all customer touchpoints. Make sure you have a full view of the customer experience. If you don't, you will risk breakdowns in service that will hurt business for sure.

Show Your Customers You're Human

You must do your best to identify shared interests with the customers you help. By humanizing your relationship, resolving any conflict will be easier and your customers will like you and your business more.

Customer Service

Listen Carefully

When you listen actively, your customers feel like you heard them. Make sure they know you understand them by clarifying and rephrasing what they said. You must empathize with them and reflect their feelings.

Admit Your Mistakes

When you mess up, admit it, even if you discover your mistakes before your customers do. Admitting you are capable of making a mistake builds trust and allows your customer's confidence to rest in your service. It also allows you to control the situation and fix the problem.

Follow Up After a Problem Is Resolved

Follow up with your customers to ensure that their issues were resolved to their satisfaction. You must be clear that they received the resolution they were looking for. Give them a call, send them an email, or offer a feedback survey. This is a great way to let your customers know you care and you're on their side.

Get Personal

Your customers want help from real people, not just your website or social media posts. Take advantage of social media (Facebook, Twitter, and review sites) and respond when your customers post on your page. Social media is about engagement and exposure, so take advantage of this to get personal with your customers. Show them the real

A Vendor's Guide to Success: How to Go from $0–$100k

side of you and your team, both on social media and on your website.

Be Accessible

Part of the personal touch is availability and accessibility. You must make it easy for your customers to reach you and your team. Even if your business is largely online, try to create opportunities for customers to see and meet you online or in person where appropriate. The more ways you are accessible (via phone, chat, text, email, etc.), the more trust you'll build with your customers.

Give the VIP Treatment

Make sure you're meeting your customers' needs. Consider offering VIP specials for your best customers to make them feel appreciated. You can create special groups for your VIPs and give them special pricing and discounts.

Create a Customer Network

A great way to make your customers feel valued is to create a sense of community around your product, which will give you a tribe of loyal supporters. You can bring your customers together for webinars, interactive websites, social media, blog comments, shows, and conferences. And even though your customers come to these forums to learn from you, it's a great opportunity for you to learn from them. I have a VIP community and a text community that allows me to connect with my customers on a deeper level.

Customer Service

Collect Customer Feedback in a Customer Friendly Way

The key to improving your customer service and growing your business is to learn about your customers' good, bad, and ugly experiences. No matter how on top of it you are, it's impossible to get in front of every issue. The best thing you can do is create multiple easily accessible touchpoints to collect customer feedback.

Know Your Customers

There's no substitute for knowing who your customers are. Take time to connect with them so you know why they are buying your product and what they love or hate about your company/products. So many business owners take their customers for granted. You need your customers! You can learn so much from them. You wouldn't have a brand if you didn't have these folks around to support it. But dig deeper. Do you know what they think of your company? Do you simply offer a quick solution to their identified need, or are they a long-standing customer? Or are they in it for you? Because you represent what they value?

You can learn a lot by understanding your customers' perception of your brand. And remember, perception is reality in the world of branding. So, you should certainly be building your customer's perception into your brand strategy.

Sometimes you will feel connected to your customers, and other times you will feel disconnected. What happens when you and your customer are simply not aligned? Who takes precedence? Do you stay true to your brand or true to your customer? It is important to stay true to both. Stay true to your brand but recognize when your customers may be feeling a bit of a disconnect. And then re-connect with them without changing the core foundation of who you are.

Communicate Clearly and Concisely

How you communicate with your customers is essential. Make sure they can understand what you are trying to convey. Watch out for passive-aggressive language ("Actually…"). This could confuse and turn off your customers. Also, avoid using slang, colloquialisms, or technical jargon.

Don't Be Rude and Stiff

When you communicate with your customers, be personable and, most importantly, be friendly. Don't treat them as if they are a number by acting like you don't care. Also, don't use an overly formal tone, as this can be a turnoff. Please make sure your team members don't come across as robots. Have real conversations with your customers.

Don't Use Negative Language

Here's an example of negative language in a customer support setting: "I can't get you an upgrade until next month. "That item is on back-order and unavailable right now."

Customer Service

Always Use Positive Language

Using positive language can change the tone of customer interaction. All team members must honor this as they deal with customers. Here's an example of positive language in a customer support setting: "That size and color will be available next month. I can put in an order for you right now and make sure you receive a notification when it arrives." In the same scenario, you could have said, "That size and color is not available, and I don't know when it will be in." Do you see the difference?

Solve Problems Quickly

One of the best ways to keep customers happy and be seen as a business that provides outstanding service is to be proactive about solving problems. In other words, solve your customers' problems the first time they present them. Your customers will appreciate you for making them a priority.

You and your team need to stay consistent in the tone you use and the processes you practice.

— Identify the problem and work to solve it so the customer leaves happy

— Acknowledge and be transparent about the issue at hand

— Refocus the discussion for a positive resolve

— Always stay in control of the situation

A Vendor's Guide to Success: How to Go from $0–$100k

Close Conversations Correctly

Every conversation with a customer should end with you saying something like, "Can I do anything else for you? I'm happy to help!" and your customer saying, "Yes, I'm all set!" When you correctly close a conversation, it shows your customers three important things:

— You care about getting things right.

— You're willing to keep going until you get things right.

— The customer is the one who decides what's "right."

Celebrate Customers with a Thank You and Appreciation

Nothing says thank you like a handwritten note. Taking the time to send a personal thank you, not via email, direct message, or inbox, can make your customers feel special. This unexpected gesture helps you build strong customer relationships. For VIP customers, throwing extra goodies in their orders creates a nice touch. Customer appreciation goes a long way in building a healthy customer relationship.

Always Remember That Customer Service Is Everyone's Responsibility

Everyone on your team should feel the burden of customer service. When your whole team is encouraged to be

Customer Service

involved in customer service, has knowledge of problems, and knows how to resolve those problems, then your customers' overall experiences will be enhanced. Taking this approach will be sure to drive your business forward. It's so simple yet often overlooked. Make sure you and your team make time to talk to customers.

Excellent customer service creates loyal customers for life who are willing to refer your business to friends, family, and colleagues. Providing this type of excellent customer service starts with a genuine desire to satisfy your customers. This is not just about selling good products but your customers' overall experiences. Your priority must be to consider their cumulative experience when they encounter your brand, what they think and feel, and what you can do to make it better. You must be in tune with learning more about your customers to create a pattern of excellent service in your business

Below, you will find some areas to focus on and always make your top priority. Others have room for growth, but these areas must be always in operation and in an upward motion. If you perfect these, you will retain loyal customers who will stick with you through thick and thin.

A Vendor's Guide to Success: How to Go from $0–$100k

1. Know Your Product or Service

To provide good customer service, you need to know what your products or services are inside and out. Make sure you and your customer-facing staff know how your products or services work. Be aware of the most common questions customers ask and know how to articulate the answers that will leave them satisfied.

2. Be Friendly

Customer Service starts with your non-verbal communication—a smile. In person, the first thing your customers should hear when they ask for help is a warm hello and greeting. Even when handling customer service requests via social media, a smile can come through in your voice, so make sure you're always friendly.

3. Say Thank You

Gratitude can go a long way, and it can remind your customers why they are shopping with you. Regardless of your business type, saying thank you after every transaction is one of the easiest ways to enhance excellent good customer service.

4. Train Your Team

It's important to make sure that all your employees, not just your customer service representatives, understand how they should talk to, interact with, and otherwise assist customers. Provide employee training that

Customer Service

gives your staff the tools they need to carry good service through the entire customer experience. Remember, you are in business for yourself, but not by yourself. I have built my team on the shoulders of my family and friends. When I first started, I couldn't afford to hire people, so my family and friends stepped in and made sure I was covered. I know everyone wants a big team, the "dream team." However, it is just not the reality for many small businesses, at least not when you first start up. The key to a successful team is making sure you have the right people at the right time. The worst thing you can do, which can be cancerous to your business, is allow people to operate in spaces they aren't strong in. You must identify what you don't do well and identify team members who can fill those gaps. For example, my sister is gifted in administration and helps me behind the scenes. I need her on my team because administration is not one of my strengths.

While my sister is gifted in administration, she would never get on a Facebook or Instagram Live and sell jewelry. However, I would because being social on social media is one of my strengths.

Therefore, it is so important for you to put people in the right areas based on their strengths. If you don't like social media, find a younger niece or nephew who can help you in that area.

A Vendor's Guide to Success: How to Go from $0–$100k

You may have a potential team member who you know is horrible with interacting with people, and this is certainly not the person you want to charge with interacting with your customers. This would be a recipe for disaster. Don't just put people in places because they are willing. It will likely mess up a lot of stuff. And if things are going to get messed up, then you should have just done it yourself.

At this point, why do you even have a team if you are doing everything yourself? You don't want people mishandling your customers. This is critical, even if family and friends are helping you. You must make sure they are fully aware of what you expect them to do and how you expect them to do it.

5. Show Respect

Customer service often can involve emotions, so it's important to make sure you and your customer service representatives are always courteous and respectful. Never let your own emotions overtake your desire to see your customer walk away happy.

6. Be Responsive

Nothing is worse than being unresponsive to a customer trying to get help, resolve an issue, or find out more about what you're selling. You must respond quickly to all inquiries, even if it is only to say you are looking into the issue and will be back in touch. Some

Customer Service

response is always better than none, so the customer doesn't feel ignored.

7. Ask for Feedback

When you ask your customers what they think of your business, products, and services, you may be surprised by what you learn about them and their needs. You can use customer surveys, feedback forms, and questionnaires, but you also can make it a common practice to ask customers first-hand for feedback when they are completing their orders.

8. Use Feedback You Receive

You need to do something with the feedback you receive from customers to make it useful. Take time to regularly review feedback, identify areas for improvement, and make specific changes in your business. Excellent customer service often comes down to consistently checking in with your customers and making sure they are happy with your products and services and the process of purchasing, ordering, and working with you. If you do that successfully, you are on your way to becoming known for providing excellent customer service.

A Vendor's Guide to Success: How to Go from $0–$100k

Capture any thoughts and comments you have after reading this chapter. How will this chapter help you?

CHAPTER 5

The Power of Your Unique Factor

Understanding your true unique factor starts with understanding your unique selling point. The unique selling point should be at the forefront of your mind, as it is the backbone of your business and brand. You should also keep this in mind when you start planning your business and even when you begin to expand. To give yourself a fighting chance, you need to stand out from the crowd.

Knowing your unique selling point is very important for every entrepreneur. It doesn't necessarily have anything to do with the design of your product, although that could be what attracts your customer base to your items. It could be your amazing ideas for customer service or even your reliability and convenience. Have you discovered an incredible material or item and hope to combine it with a special product or fabric? Or maybe your bag brand solves a problem for the consumer. Whatever direction you choose, try

A Vendor's Guide to Success: How to Go from $0–$100k

not to offer too much, as you will then be remembered for just blending into the already overcrowded market.

The best way to find **perfect customers** and create new ones is by identifying your Unique Factor.

Use these key selling points and communicate these key benefits to all your customers.

Key 1—Market Placement

When you plan to start a business or product line, finding your place in the market is number one. Does your business or product have a place? If your answer is yes, then how does it differentiate itself and appear unique?

It's **OK to be like a business or product that already exists** and is doing well; just make sure people know how your business and product are unique.

Getting customers to buy your product and support your business can be challenging and will require work on your part. You will need to make sure it is properly placed and has the right kind of face time with the public. If your product or business is brand new and unique, how do you establish it in the market?

Key 2—Price Points

Do you sell products of quality at affordable prices? Do you sell luxury one-of-a-kind items? The answers to these questions will determine how expensive or cheap your products are. And remember, there are customers on each side. You just need to be clear about what side

60

The Power of Your Unique Factor

your business is on. Use your "market analysis" to identify your price point to avoid under or overpricing your products and services. Be sure to include the total manufacturing overhead costs incurred to determine your total product costs.

Key 3—After the Sale Service

Handling your customers after the sale is just as important as securing the sale. Once you have sold items, it's a great idea to offer customers some kind of service and support. It's an excellent way to share your brand values. This will help you build brand loyalty and ensure changing customers from first-timers to repeat customers. Make sure they are clear about your return policies and don't make it challenging for them. Customers love to buy from places that have customer-friendly return policies. You will find that people will buy more when they feel that your return policy is not complicated.

Knowing where you stand in the market will enable you to launch a social media campaign that targets your customers directly. You will spend the most on the development and manufacture of your items, so have some finances in place to achieve this.

Getting all these points right will ensure that you give yourself a head start in such a competitive arena. Don't forget that building something new takes time and a lot of hard work. Try to let things evolve naturally and, most importantly, enjoy the journey.

61

A Vendor's Guide to Success: How to Go from $0–$100k

Have you discovered what differentiates your content and why it's harder than ever for brands to be "unique"? Here's some food for thought for entrepreneurs that I live by:

1. You need fortitude.
2. Establish a solid faith walk with GOD.
3. Sometimes you will make money; sometimes you will not.
4. Even when you do your due diligence, you may not make money.
5. Be willing to stick with it.
6. Don't be in it for a quick buck.
7. Are people paying for the event or is it a free show? Customers coming to a free event are on a different level than those paying a fee.
8. Assess the fee for the show.
9. Look at how much you pay and bump it up based on how long you can sell because you may not have enough time to make money and even recoup what you paid.
10. Ideally, you are in proximity with all attendees, etc.
11. You don't want to be tucked in a corner.

The Power of Your Unique Factor

12. Go online and check out who is following the host; that will tell you your audience.

13. Make sure your product fits the type of event. For example, you should not be showcasing at a flea market if you sell high-end jewelry.

14. I learned the hard way. At one point, I was doing shows everywhere, including a club.

15. When I did shows at the club, there was no light. How would I sell with no light?

16. Make sure that time, effort, and energy are not wasted.

17. Put a dollar figure on your time, effort, and energy.

18. I also must pay staff at times.

19. You may be better off saving your money for the big events like the $500 event versus going with $25 or $50 events.

20. Determine what's best for you. Everything is not for everyone.

21. FB Lives are trending for showing products, but it's not for everyone.

22. Be consistent in the quality of your product and visual presentation. Don't have your customers on a roller coaster—one day your products are good and the other they are bad. This is not good for your brand.

A Vendor's Guide to Success: How to Go from $0–$100k

23. Add organically to your brand. If you sell jewelry, you shouldn't start selling barbecue sauce. This is brand confusion. Stay in your lane, especially when just starting out. It's okay to add to your brand. For example, if you sell necklaces, you can add earrings. It makes sense because it's in the jewelry family. Always add products that you yourself use and wear every day and have personal testimonies to back them up.

The Power of Your Unique Factor

Capture any thoughts and comments you have after reading this chapter. How will this chapter help you?

CHAPTER 6

The Setup

Setting up your booth, table or backdrop for an event can be tricky. Many people think they know what to do and how to make their booth/event space appealing to the customer, and most times, they get it wrong. Your setup is everything at live events or conferences, but always adapt it to the venue where you are showcasing.

I do a major outdoor show in Columbia, Maryland every year, rain or shine. I am typically prepared for anything that comes my way. I have tent walls for rain, stakes to hold the tent firmly down, and plastic shelving that can easily be wiped down since it's an outdoor show. Well, this year, I was not ready for the monsoon that came! The heavens opened and rain came from the north, south, and east! It was crazy. I had help with me

A Vendor's Guide to Success: How to Go from $0–$100k

as we tried to bring the tent in all types of ways to help with just the droves and drives of water. It was a sight to see!

I had to adapt my setup immediately—take jewelry off my beautiful new stand I had just purchased, lay the jewelry flat on the table, take purses and clothing from hanging up high for display and put on the regular clothing rack, and even put some items away, as they were beginning to get damaged. These are the type of stories all business owners will have, so just be ready!

Now let's look at some pointers for booth/event space setup to help you maximize your space and attract customers to your table.

Setting Up for a Show

If you are just starting to plan your first show, you'll want to think seriously about how to set up your table and space. It seems that the most important part of show preparation is making sure your products are displayed well. If not, it will be hard to entice customers to buy. Below is a brief list of things you may want to consider as a minimum in setting up your display.

The Setup

1. Use a plain colored tablecloth that goes to the floor

2. Match table coverings to your logo or company colors

3. Create different levels or tiers on the table

4. Use stands and holders as opposed to laying things flat on the table

5. Provide a mirror for customers when trying pieces on

6. Add proper signage for business names, payments accepted, and policies

Tablecloth

It's nice if your cloth is made of fabric that will not wrinkle. Use tablecloths where wrinkles shake out nicely even if you don't fold it well following a show. The color you use can depend on the type of show and the look you want to achieve. You use a second covering over a cloth. Ensure your cloth is long enough to reach the floor to properly hide all your materials under the table. Your cloth can be part of a theme that you have identified. Table coverings should also match your logo or company colors. If not defined yet, I suggest using black or white to start.

Display Levels/Tiers

Create different levels or tiers on top of your table to add character and provide more room for your display.

A Vendor's Guide to Success: How to Go from $0–$100k

You can place empty boxes under the tablecloth or utilize decorative items to place jewelry on. For example, interesting small wooden crates or upside-down baskets can be used. Some vendors raise the entire table by placing PVC pipe on each table leg. They want to help raise the jewelry to prevent customers from bending over the table. If you try this, be sure that the table is stable enough that it won't fall when someone leans on it.

Commercial jewelry display items are readily available online and at some jewelry shows. These are usually covered in black or velvet. If you want a different look, you can make some of the display items. Picture frames may be converted to necklace holders by attaching small nails or hooks in the top back for securing the jewelry that hangs in front of the frame. Also, using leather jewelry stands helps you to stand out and give a different look. Using benching tables to create levels is ideal as well.

Mirrors

At a minimum, provide a mirror for your customers. Many women will want to see how the necklace looks around their own neck. I also use several flat mirrors throughout my display, either under pieces on the table or leaning against a tier. You may think this is simple, but I can't tell you how many times other jewelry vendors ask to borrow my mirror. It would amaze you. Hang small mirrors near as many of your displays as you can and

The Setup

include one larger mirror for those who want to get the full effect of the products people try on.

Also, different types of glassware can be used to effectively display different items. For example, you can place mirrors under the glasses for a different presentation. Tiered shelving draped in fabric can also be effective for displays.

Booth Personality—TABLE SETUP

First and foremost, you must be consistent when it comes to table setup, as it will make or break your sales bottom line. Your table's overall visual must be clutter-free. This is probably the most important tip I can give you. Why? If it is cluttered and you have too much going on, people will not be attracted to your table. It can be over-stimulating for your customers. Don't have your product jumbled up, and please make sure your items are layered neatly. This allows your customers to easily view and access what is on your table. Please don't just throw your products in containers or trays because it will look unprofessional.

You want your customers to clearly see everything on your table. It doesn't just apply to jewelry but also candles, clothing, shea butter, etc. No matter what product you are selling, you must have a clutter-free setup. You should also have some height and elevation on your table, which gives some dimension to your presentation.

A Vendor's Guide to Success: How to Go from $0–$100k

Even if you are selling books, you still need elevation. I can't tell you how many author's tables I have seen with their books just lying flat on the table. They are missing so many sales because people aren't drawn to it. On the other hand, I have seen author's tables with height elevation who have people standing in line to purchase their book.

Elevation adds so much value to a table. You could sell lip gloss and lipstick; it doesn't matter because you still need elevation when displaying on a table.

You can create elevation with boxes with table clothes on top of benches. This is important because you want a table that is pleasing to the eye and will draw people. So many people often tell me that my tables are cute. They like the idea of a nice table, and it prompts them to stop by. Then amazing customer service gets them to buy. You can also use clear stackable containers to create an elevated look for your table. Branded signage should be part of the elevated look as well. On another note, Amazon will be your friend, especially for those in the vending space. Amazon has all types of plastic containers and things for signage and various displays. You can get your containers, table cloths, runners, and anything else you need.

Also, when people come to your "nice" table, please make sure you speak to them and engage with them. That is so important. The minute people come to your table, it is showtime. I have been at so many shows where vendors barely speak to people who take the time to come to their

The Setup

tables. If you are on your phone when someone walks up, get your head out from your phone, stand up if you can, and speak. No one will want to engage you if you are mean. Not only is it rude, but it says that you don't want to sell anything. Why are you there if you don't want to talk to people and engage with them. Engagement on every level is important for entrepreneurs. This goes for both live and online events. When you engage with people, you can secure new customers and retain current customers.

People like to know if those they buy from are relatable, especially for in-person shopping experiences. You must be warm, cheerful, inviting, welcoming, and inviting. You need to provide service with a smile, which I would say I have mastered.

If you have too much product to display at one time, put some items beneath your table. You should never feel pressured to put everything out at one time because it will compromise the integrity of what you are showcasing. You will also have to identify your standard configuration for your ideal setup.

When I determined that I needed two tables to have my perfect setup, I stuck with that. I was so committed to my setup that I would not showcase at shows or events that would not allow me to have two tables. If you ever face this dilemma, you can decide to downsize your product offering to fit on just one table.

A Vendor's Guide to Success: How to Go from $0–$100k

Now, I know you may be thinking it is not a big deal and I am too picky. It is a big deal today because setup is everything. I have seen people not sell anything because their tables were not set up properly. Over the years, I have mastered table setup, and I attribute much of my sales over the years to having the right setup. For vendors, the proper table setting is everything. It is like a window display for a department store and requires attention and intentionality. This is an area that I have cultivated and have grown in over the years. And this is one of the reasons why some business owners hire me to be their consultant. Yes, I help business owners with table setup because it is essential for those in the vending space.

At this point in my business, I don't set up at shows or events if I can't have two tables. I know what I need to be my best self in the vending space, and it entails two tables.

Now that we have covered how you should display your product, let's talk about how the table should be covered. You should always use a higher-end tablecloth because it gives a more polished and professional look. Identify a color scheme and align your tablecloth with that. If you can't come up with something, just go with solid colors like black or white. Make sure your tablecloths match. You should not have a little bit of this color and a little bit of that color. Everything should be color coordinated. Consistency with your table linen is key.

The Setup

Never, never under any circumstances use plastic tablecloths. Plastic immediately takes the value away from your presentation. You can't have a $60 or $100 item sitting on top of a $1.00 tablecloth. That is just not a good look for several reasons.

Having a nice table with quality linen will allow you to stand out. How do you stand out at events and shows with multiple vendors? You do that by making sure you have a well-coordinated table display. I know we all get busy and want to take shortcuts and cut corners, but your table is not one of those areas where you want to cut corners. People with awesome products have paid me to design their tables because they said they were missing sales because people were not drawn to their tables. Stale tables will not draw people, but a fresh table will. Investing time in your table setup is worth your time, energy, and attention. You will thank me and yourself later.

One additional touch that you may want to consider adding to your overall table presentation is music, depending on the show type. Now, I am not talking about blasting your favorite hype music. I am talking about some soft jazz music that you can play at a low level. I have seen people add music to their tables.

I typically don't play music at my table unless it's soft jazz instrumental. Depending on the show type, you should adjust your music accordingly. If you are at a Christian women's conference, I am sure it is not a problem to

A Vendor's Guide to Success: How to Go from $0–$100k

have a little praise and worship music playing in the background. Most shows will spell out the protocol for music in the guidelines you receive as a vendor. Please don't go against the guidelines because you don't want to tarnish your business reputation. Be sure to check the regulations per event so that you are clear.

The information above sets the stage for your display; however, you may want to give your booth a specific personality.

Lighting

Many vendors add lights to their display area. These can be helpful depending on the setting for the show. Vendors usually pay extra to have electricity in their booths. If you are selling jewelry and clothing, I highly suggest always traveling with extra lighting because it makes a huge difference. Subtle lighting that's flattering to people's faces when they try on something in front of a mirror is critical, and it's easy to display some of your products in a lightbox. Bring battery-operated lights where access to electricity is a problem, such as at outdoor events.

Take a Good Look at Your Display

When you finish setting up your display, stand back and act like a customer. Is this a place where you would want to stop and consider making a purchase? Does the display contain so much that it is difficult to discern what is available? I realize that less may be more, and the customer's

The Setup

eye does need somewhere to stop rather than just viewing too many pieces. Now I keep extra jewelry beneath the table. If a customer is interested in a particular style or color, I can then pull out anything I've kept below. When I do this, the customer often feels quite special.

Extras

These may not be display items but can certainly help you maintain your display. You should have a lint roller for cleaning the displays. This is particularly helpful on velvet display pieces and black tablecloths. You may also want to carry a glass cleaning product and cleaning cloth to help keep mirrors and glass displays clean and immaculate. I now have a hardware bin of cleaning products and odds and ends just in case, such as safety pins, tape, bungee cords, hammers, nails, heavy-duty tape, etc.

When I first started selling accessories, I had a very elaborate display. It took over two-plus hours to set everything up and another two hours to take it all down again after a show.

I began streamlining my display a bit more after each show to make it simpler. I finally sat down and made a **list of what I needed** and came up with the setup I use now. When renting a booth to sell at a show, it's important to encourage people to buy pieces on the spot while making it possible for customers to buy more once the show ends. Creating an eye-catching booth/table is the first step in attracting buyers. Whether everything is displayed on one

A Vendor's Guide to Success: How to Go from $0–$100k

table or on several stands in a roomy, walk-in space, creating an uncluttered display that encourages browsing is key to making sales.

Giveaways

Offer a beautiful item as a grand prize to those who put their names and contact information, such as phone number, email, or mailing address, into a big bowl. Display the winning item in your area, along with signage about the drawing, to encourage people to enter. Send your new contacts a marketing email and mention the winner of the drawing to build interest and remind them of the products you sell.

Digital Collateral Materials for Displays

Hand out a colorful postcard or flyer with photos of some of your best products. Include your website address, and if you provide a shopping cart on the site, mention a discount on certain items when they shop online. Offer an "after event special." For example, you can give 30% off one item.

Be mindful that the display design, the lighting, and the decoration of the surrounding area can attract paying customers who will become repeat customers.

The more attractive and eye-catching your display is, the more prospective customers you're likely to attract. Make sure your display represents your brand and gives a clear view of everything you are selling. Displays are

The Setup

effective visual tools that help business owners present their products in public spaces. Using designed custom product tags can aid in catching the customers' eye.

Selling in Spaces with Competition

After setting up at shows, I often saw other vendors with the same or similar items. I used to stress out about that. I don't at this point because it is what it is. You can ask the event host if moving to another space is an option. If it's not, then keep it moving. Your price is your price, so don't change it because someone else has it. Base your price on how much you paid for the items and how much you want to make. When you remain consistent with your pricing, people with remain loyal to you. Occasionally, vendors have asked me to increase my price for an item to match their products, and I kindly declined. It is important for me to maintain pricing consistency.

Stay true to what you sell. Let customers buy where they want to buy because they have the right to do so. Don't let it get the best of you, and don't try to steal customers from other people. It is just not worth it. People have still purchased from me in these scenarios because they like my table, they like how I greet them, and they like how my items are displayed. Sometimes I put my jewelry on mannequins, and it captures the attention of potential customers. As long as you remain confident in what you have to offer, the customers will come.

A Vendor's Guide to Success: How to Go from $0–$100k

Please don't get distracted and start panicking. I am not telling you not to do the competitive analysis taught in business school, which you should do when you are first launching your business. In a vendor situation, you have time to do a deep analysis. You may miss sales if you are focus on trying to shift and see what other vendors have.

If you have wiggle room, then you can adjust. Just don't do it out of pressure. You must be confident in your brand and what you are offering.

Selling Online—Doing Facebook and IG Lives

Before we dive into how to do a virtual show, let's quickly go over what it is. Basically, it's a way to sell your products from your home, even if you don't have an online store. It's an alternative to selling your jewelry on a platform such as **Etsy** or selling on your own website. Usually, there's some sort of live element, meaning that the selling happens in real-time.

So, should you do Lives? Ask yourself the following questions:

1. Do I have a vibrant personality?
2. Do I have an extreme amount of patience?
3. Can I be engaging when reading comments and showing products?

The Setup

4. Can I stay on track for one to three hours of selling my products?

5. Do I have a team to help me?

6. Do I have enough inventory to offer customers?

7. How will I ship?

8. Do I have rules of purchase?

9. Do I have the capacity and infrastructure to handle Lives (even at home)?

10. Can I handle the volume of business?

11. If you answered yes to all the questions continue. If you cannot, doing Lives may not be for you.

At the time of writing this book, the world is experiencing the COVID-19 pandemic and many in-person events aren't even possible. Online live events are a nice alternative to selling at a vending show or event, given the times we are in.

Some benefits include:

- You can do it anywhere at any time.

- There's no need to spend money to set up your home.

- If you're new to selling, it's a way to get your foot in the door.

- It has little to no cost (except for your time).

- It's a way to sell off inventory that you want to move.

A Vendor's Guide to Success: How to Go from $0–$100k

HOW TO HOST A VIRTUAL SHOW...EVEN IF YOU'VE NEVER SOLD ONLINE BEFORE

Here's the exact step-by-step process I used to host my own online jewelry trunk show.

Before you host the event, here are some steps you should take to help ensure it is a success.

Gather information about the products you're selling

- **Take photos of all your products**—While these don't necessarily have to be the best product photos, especially if you decide to show off the products via video during the event, I do recommend you edit your photos, either using the software that comes loaded on your phone or computer or using an online platform or app.

- **Write out the product description**—Keep descriptions simple and include information about sizing.

- **Price your products**—Unless you're selling old inventory that you're tired of looking at, please don't underprice your work.

- Have a place where you collect all your research and product information. You can use a folder or hard drive on your computer. You can also capture pictures and store them on your phone.

The Setup

Figure out shipping

Will you do flat-rate shipping, or will it be per weight? Will you ship internationally or domestically? I decided to simplify things by shipping online in the U.S., where I reside, and using flat-rate shipping. (I charge $5 no matter how many pieces people purchase.)

Choose a payment processor

Customers need a way to pay you! If you have a business already set up, you should be able to create invoices in whatever platform you use to collect payments.

Decide how the virtual live show will proceed & establish the rules

The first time I did a live show, I numbered items and had a full program that included giveaways.

The event proceeded as follows:

- I created the buzz, promoted my Lives on social media, and encouraged everyone to share and join the event.

- During the event, I showed each item with a corresponding number and requested that each person comment if they wanted to buy.

- I had several trivia questions and door prizes for customers to win throughout the show to encourage people to invite people and interact with the event. The door prizes are usually small discounts good for the Live only.

- People who purchased had a couple of hours to pay their invoices; otherwise, any piece they wanted to purchase went to the next person on the list who expressed interest.

Create the virtual show event & share with your networks

I created flyers to post on my page. I also use **Canva** (they have fantastic templates) or hire a graphic designer to create images for the event. I invite friends and family who might be interested and encourage them to invite people.

Leading up to the event

In the week or so leading up to the event, drum up excitement:

- Post flyer and albums of the pieces of what I am selling
- Share images periodically on social media pages
- Post countdown reminders on the event page itself
- Keep posting. People forget, so just keep posting

Resources for hosting a live show

Hopefully, you have received some great virtual ideas after reading this. Here are some resources for hosting an online show

- **Canva** or creating graphics
- **PicMonkey** for editing videos

The Setup

- **Square, Cash App, Venmo,** or **Zelle** for accepting payment
- **XPS, Ship, Shipping Easy,** or **Pirate Ship** for e-commerce shipping

Here are some additional tips to help you have a successful live online show.

- Start preparing weeks in advance.
- Choose your platform and practice on it.
- Consider a theme. Make it fun.
- Have good photography, videography, and lighting; use a ring light.
- Script your discussion.
- Offer incentives, such as giveaways, to attend and stay through the end.
- Practice speaking in front of a mirror.
- Be energetic.

Always Plan the Best Time for the Event

Like any successful event, shows takes planning. Whether you are doing it once a year or once a week, it requires planning. After all, you want to be showing new and unique merchandise that is worth the full price, not sales items. Determine whether the show will be an exclusive one-day, after-hours event or whether it will run over several days. If you have enough potential customers for a private event, this may be the way to go.

A Vendor's Guide to Success: How to Go from $0–$100k

However, if you're looking to the show to help determine if a new line is good for your business, a three- or four-day event will reach more customers and give you a better idea of how your products present themselves to your customer base.

Promote, Promote, Promote

A show will never be successful without strong promotion. Several weeks before, start promoting the event. Share flyers or post, post, post and have your network share. Create large full-colored posters for your tables if you are at a show. Create an event on your Facebook or IG page. Keep posting about the event in the weeks and days beforehand. By posting on both yours and the vendor's social media sites, you reach double the audience. Feature the event prominently on your website, along with some background on the artist and perhaps a short video about the products.

Send email announcements to your customers and follow up with a second email. People need more than one impression to remember something.

If the show will be a private event, analyze your customer database for the key customers to invite. Choose those customers who have purchased similar items in the past, have generally paid full price for items, or who typically attend your events. Don't waste the effort on someone who only shops occasionally and then only when you have sales.

The Setup

Truly Make It an Exciting Event

Be energetic, make jokes, and engage with customers. Have a proper backdrop, and make it look like you are at an on-site event. The customer should see no difference.

Price Appropriately

A show is an exclusive event, not just another sale. As such, the pricing should reflect this. Don't offer discounted merchandise. Instead, consider noting in the marketing materials and signage that items are "specially priced for the live event." This gives the impression that customers are getting a deal but doesn't specify a certain percentage off or sale amount. While many customers will purchase items at the full price for a chance to buy something truly unique, others might still be looking for a bargain.

Follow Up for Success

During the event, encourage customers to follow your page to stay informed of your live shows, discounts, and new arrivals. Encourage them to share and spread the word! Thank them for participating. You will have to repeat yourself over and over during any live sale, so get used to it. That's where extreme patience comes in. You will be ok. Online Lives are great and can be a very profitable venture, right from your own home.

A Vendor's Guide to Success: How to Go from $0–$100k

Capture any thoughts and comments you have after reading this chapter. How will this chapter help you?

CHAPTER 7

Lessons Learned

I learned so many lessons regarding vending. Let me share some of the major ones with you to shave off some pain and prevent you from experiencing what I have over the years. Many business owners lose money because of bad vending decisions. Check out some of my lessons learned over the years:

Lesson 1: Show Selection

Show selection is one of the biggest pitfalls for business owners. I have personally experienced this one over the years, and it has cost me a lot of time, money, inventory, and resources. First, you just can't say yes to every vending opportunity you are presented with. You must do some investigative work on the front end. I have seen so many new entrepreneurs who are zealous about showcasing their products and have such enthusiasm that it clouds their vision. I know that new business owners want to get their products out to as many people as possible and think

A Vendor's Guide to Success: How to Go from $0–$100k

vending is the way to do it. It can cost you greatly if you don't pick the right vending event, and you could end up frustrated and disappointed.

You have costs associated with the event, staff, and inventory. A few things will be important as you consider what show you should select—scrutinize everything!

Below are some critical questions you must ask before you commit and pay any required deposits.

1. How are they advertising the event? Do they have flyers? Will they be promoted on all social platforms? Do they have radio or TV press?

2. If it is a church event, ask how many people are in the congregation and the expected attendance.

3. How many do you have registered?

4. Where will the vendors be placed? Sometimes I paid for an event and the vendors were in a completely different building. We had to make people cross the street. This put pressure on me to convince customers to walk across the street to see my goods. Even give incentives and giveaways to encourage them to come over to where the vendors were set up. Although an event host will say that they will let people know where vendors are located, they often get caught up and forget to mention the vendors. In the

90

Lessons Learned

virtual space, you must know the platforms being used and how much time you have.

5. Where will I be placed? If you are placed in an area away from the activities or other vendors, it will be hard for people to see you. This puts you at a huge disadvantage.

Lesson 2: Be Selective with the Show Host

It is so easy to make the mistake of choosing an event based on a person's popularity. I have done it myself.

They may have many people following them on social media, but it does not mean they will host an event that is right for you. I have seen many well-known people on social media host events and have a low turnout.

A low turnout for a vending can be a nightmare, but it can also be a joyous occasion depending on who is in the room. That is why you must be very selective. A small group of the right people could be a big night of sales for you. You could also have a very large event with the wrong people and make no money.

Lesson 3: Do Your Research and Due Diligence

Check out the host. A great flyer doesn't mean their event will have a great response. Many people can be false positives on social media. All the research will allow you to see what can be potentially yielded from the event.

Check out their social media pages and any digital platforms they use. If you don't see the event flyer on the host page, that is a red flag. Ultimately, vending can be risky. Nothing is guaranteed! It is an absolute faith walk. This is why you must do your due diligence. Although I want you to go into every event hopeful and with an open mind, you must still operate in wisdom.

Lesson 4: Know Your Audience

Make sure you set up at events that align with your audience. For example, if you sell men's accessories, you may not want to set up at a women's conference. While women may buy things for the special men in their lives, it is still a women's event.

Lesson 6: Take Time for Yourself

Always remember if you are not healthy, you will be no good to yourself and others. You must make yourself a priority in the midst of family, friends, and your business pulling from you. It can be taxing, and you want to be your best for your current and potential customers. On many occasions over the years, I was burning the candlestick at both ends and my health was compromised. During those times, I had to take a pause, vacation, and focus on getting well. I have learned over the years to make time for myself on a regular basis so that I am not forced to do it because my body shuts down. As I said before, you must have

Lessons Learned

tough skin as an entrepreneur. It can also be very draining and can weigh on your mind, body, and spirit. Being in business can be a lonely road, but it is worth the reward of the success you can experience.

Lesson 7: Investing in Yourself and Business

Investing in myself and my business is a priority for me. I have a mentor because it's important for me to be poured into by someone who can take me to the next level. And for those who I have mentored, it is important to me that they know I have a mentor. You should not have a mentor who is not being mentored by someone. Everyone, and I mean everyone, needs a mentor. I also make sure that I invest in quality products for Jewels By Joan 2. You may have to start off small or with low-quality products, but it shouldn't remain that way. That is why you must invest back into your business. Please don't use what you earn to get your hair done or pay your rent. If that is the case, then you should not be a full-time entrepreneur. You may need to get a 9 to 5 as a jump start and a financial supplement until you expand. I invest in my image and my brand because that is so important. If I want people to buy my quality product at a certain price point, I must look the part. Having a line item in the budget for hair, nails, and clothing is critical. Depending on the industry, your outfit could be considered your "uniform." You must do the things needed to be successful. If you want to go to the next level, you must get

A Vendor's Guide to Success: How to Go from $0–$100k

with people who want to max out. You may have to invest in that high-end event to get your name out there. That is a form of investment.

Lesson 7: Make the Customer Experience Everything

People buy experiences, so you need to invest in the total package. What do I mean by experience? I mean what people get from you when they experience your business, from the packaging to the website, to your postcard. It is all an investment. You may not think paying for tissue paper for your bags or boxes is necessary, but if it adds value to the overall presentation, then you may want to invest in it. You may not initially have the budget for the bells and whistles but start at your level and work your way up.

See what your competition is doing and do more and better. You must create the advantage for yourself, especially when you are in a saturated industry or selling the same thing as someone else. What will make them purchase from you? It will be the overall experience and presentation. If you don't want to invest in yourself or your business, you're saying you don't want to grow or evolve. When your business grows, you may have to invest in different equipment and software. You will have to consistently invest back into your business and yourself. You may have to hire consultants to do certain things that you can't do. Paying someone will shave off your to-do list and free

Lessons Learned

up time for you to be the face of your brand. When your business grows, you may decide to create an extension of your brand to create new products, etc. You will need to have start-up money for that, which is an investment. Don't get stuck on one level of success and say you are good. You should never just be "good" with a level of success. It should be your desire to keep excelling and growing. And that will only happen when you truly invest in yourself and your business.

I recommend consistently reinvesting in branding, quality product, mentorship, coaching, and vacationing. You may need to upgrade your technology and devices. If doing Lives using your phone no longer works, then you may need to get an iPad. Self-care is a non-negotiable investment to free up brain space so you can maintain your energy and creativity. Going until your body shuts down is not an investment. Get help if you need it and can afford it. Don't derail yourself or your business by trying to do everything yourself. If you are not good with keeping your finances, then hire a bookkeeper or an accountant. Eliminate the stress by procuring the services you need so that your business is efficient. I don't have an issue with staying in my lane and outsourcing.

Challenges Along the Way

The challenges I have faced over the years as an entrepreneur could be a book in itself. I have certainly had my

A Vendor's Guide to Success: How to Go from $0–$100k

fair share of barriers and brick walls. One of the biggest challenges I have faced has been jealousy and hatred from people when I decided to become a business owner and walk in a different manner than I used to. The hate comes because they are upset that you decided to be an entrepreneur and do things on your own. This could be the case for several reasons, like maybe they want to do it on their own and don't know how to, so they attempt to figure out how you did it. Some will even try to count your money. This could also happen with people on social media. It is so sad to see people operate in jealousy and hate because someone else decided to pursue their dreams and get closer to their destiny.

You can't let people distract you because you decide to go into business, operate in your God-given talents, and make some money. Don't let people count your money. I don't care who it is. People will always have some type of jealously for those who are operating in their purpose. Another challenge I have faced is not going to the right event to sell. I have traveled weekend after weekend lugging all my stuff only to not make any money. I've paid for events and didn't even make that back. Can you imagine how disappointing this was? When I mentor, this is a *big* deal for me. Depending on what you are selling, you need to be in the right environments. I have gone to clubs to sell jewelry. *Why?* There's no lighting, and people want to drink and dance, not buy jewelry. I have learned to be in the right

Lessons Learned

space to make sure I have a fighting chance to make money and properly display my products. Sometimes I wanted to showcase at an event or show but couldn't afford it. You have to do what you have to do. Sometimes you may have to negotiate with the host to see if you can pay them in payment plans or after you sell items at the event or show. I remember when I really wanted to be part of a show, but the vendor fee was $750. I barely had $7.50 to my name during that time, but I believed in my brand. Listen, I did what I needed to do. I knew that my payday was coming up, so I asked the host if I could split up the payments, and he said yes. I made the two payments on time because I believe in keeping my word. As a small business, all you have is your word and your integrity. This show ended up being one of my best shows. I was trying to figure out how to attend this show that would have 30,000 attendees. God worked it out for me and gave me favor. And just think, I didn't even have the money to pay as a vendor. While a big challenge, I made it work, I hustled, and I made payment arrangements that I stuck to and ended up making $5,500.00 for the week. That was major for me and still is!

It turns out that man had different shows worldwide, and he had no issues with allowing me to get on a payment plan for any show I wanted to participate in. I did several other events with him, and each event broadened my customer base, and I made serious money at his shows. God is so good!

A Vendor's Guide to Success: How to Go from $0–$100k

I also experienced some customer service issues. To be transparent, some customers are just wrong (they know it). I always try to make the best of the situation, but sometimes nothing will please them. You will have to suck it up most times and always take the high road. Ultimately, the potential confrontation with a customer is not worth it over a $50 purchase, or any amount for that matter.

You are better off giving them their money back so that you can have peace of mind and move on. There will be many happy and positive customers to make up for that one. Customers will also try to blast you on social media and speak ill of you with their networks. Even if you give them their money back, they may still try to speak badly about you and your business.

As long as you stand on fair customer service practices, you don't have anything to worry about. I have repeat customers that stay with me because of my customer service. My grandmother taught me so much regarding the importance of excellent customer service. Trust me; I know this can be frustrating, but you have to keep it moving. You may even have to block some customers on social media if they take their negativity too far and are just nasty. You will also encounter customers that may order things from you and don't pay their invoice. For those types of customers, you just need to have systems in place to weed them out. Please don't let them be repeat offenders. Don't let people

Lessons Learned

hold up the product and keep it away from customers who may be willing to pay.

You also want to beware of those customers who always want a discount. They don't understand that discounts won't help grow your business. It is okay to give discounts when you can. However, you initially need paying customers to actually grow your business. People should not feel like they can get a "hook up" every time they encounter you. Stay away from those people. I have also had my fair share of customers who "don't like" the products they purchased. This is often a tactic to get a refund. I don't make a big deal with those types of customers.

I give them a refund and move on. Trust me; it's not worth it. Don't get stuck on small stuff; vent your frustrations to a friend or family member and keep it moving. You must have tough skin to have longevity as an entrepreneur.

I have also experienced challenges around product quality. You order an item and it looks one way, but when you receive it, it looks different. What do you do when that happens? You can discount products and let customers know you are doing so because the quality doesn't meet your standards. They can take it or leave it. Your honesty will build trust with your customers. All you can do is try to work it out and recover. Build a buffer into your business model that will allow for sudden adjustments and modifications.

I have also faced challenges not directly connected to my business but connected to other vendors and service

A Vendor's Guide to Success: How to Go from $0–$100k

providers that I use, like web designers. They don't do your site or your business cards professionally, which is critical to your ability to share your business. Try and really vet the vendors you use for your business. Establish that you are legit and a serious business person. Always pay invoices on time. Although you can't predict how some vendors will treat you, do what you can on your side. When things like that happen, find somebody else who can accommodate your needs. In all of this, you still must push through. If you say what you are doing is your passion, you owe it to yourself to "push"!

As an entrepreneur, you will always face challenges no matter how big you grow or how much money you make. Nothing will exempt you from challenges. However, your ability to continue to push through will separate you from the weak. With each level comes a different set of challenges. Every day won't be peachy, with you singing and smelling the roses as you skip. You never just "arrive." Every level of success will give you challenges.

The key will be your ability to push through. How did you respond? How did you push through? Did you exhaust different options? You never want to be in a position where you are relying on one vendor. Get a list of multiple vendors. Do what you have to do to hold people accountable and maintain the integrity of your business. Just don't let setbacks cause you to give up. Push Through!

Lessons Learned

You must have a global brand mindset, and that is why you must stay focused. My goal is to be listed as one of Oprah's favorite things one day and give everyone a Cecilia J Collection item. This is long term for me. I am not just trying to have a side hustle. This will ultimately be my full income, which means I can't let people get in the way. I am believing God for this. When you have this kind of mindset, it is a completely different level of grind. As you lock into this mindset, you will definitely lose some friends because you will no longer be so easily accessible and available. You can't be here, there, and everywhere. You can't go to the bar or attend every social event you are invited to. Why? Because you have big goals and your dreams are counting on you to succeed and not to be distracted.

No, I can't go to that event because I have a show to prepare for. No, I can't go to that play because I have to finish writing my book. No, I can't go to happy hour because I have to go home and do my Jewels by Joan 2 Live... No! You must stay focused if you really want to go from "pushing products" into a legitimate business with a consistent track record. You must get to the place where you are no longer breaking even, but you are making a profit and can pay yourself.

People will pull you from your grind and leave you high and dry. And they will leave you broke. Please don't

A Vendor's Guide to Success: How to Go from $0–$100k

make the mistake of needing anything from them because they won't have it give to you, yet they want you to step away from your grind. Once people see you are serious, they may try to label you and make you feel bad. You may hear things like "all she wants to do is her business" or "her business has changed her." Guess what? They are right... all you want to do is your business... why? Because you have goals, and you are changed because your business is growing and thriving. You don't owe anyone an apology for your grind or success. They will pull away anyway. Lean on your true family and friends who respect your hustle and want to see you grow. Get around people who appreciate and understand your grind—like-minded individuals. These people will be willing to assist you because they see the end goal. You must be locked in even if you lose relationships. Keeping it moving doesn't mean you don't love those who don't understand you. It just means you are trying to grow without distractions. Relationships will be lost because you are on a different level.

The good news is that you will make some new friends and establish new relationships because you are on a new level. You will see God in all of it, but you must believe in Him and yourself.

You are trying to max out your business and be a household name, which comes with hard work, dedication, and focus. Jewels by Joan 2 and The Cecilia J Collection will be household names because I am not giving

Lessons Learned

up. You must keep that focused mindset. When you lose family and friends, don't take it personal. You are no longer content with what they are content with. You are not just satisfied with the norm because you are an entrepreneur. As the famous saying goes, if it was easy, everyone would be doing it! This statement holds true through the test of time.

In addition to being listed as one of Oprah's favorite things, my goal is to employ people and have a Cecilia J storefront, be a household name, and continue to grow my brand. You must see beyond where your business is currently. I see my Cecilia J signage on my storefront. I am in it to win it! And I am not playing games with anyone. You should not play games as a business owner. Do you see the future of your business as you operate in the present? As you become more focused on expanding your business and building a legacy, you will become an outlier because everyone won't have that same mindset. You must know that up front and be okay with it. Your future goals are much more important than some of the low-level things some of your friends or associates may want you to focus on. Most successful entrepreneurs or big-league companies have a serious grind, and people with that mindset will appreciate your grind.

A Vendor's Guide to Success: How to Go from $0–$100k

You have to max out your grind. I am trying to focus on generational wealth, and I am okay with those who don't think it is important. Take some time to process the disconnection, but don't get consumed by it. Once your business grows and you have a solid team, that will free you up to be with your loved ones. This will help you have balance, which is very important. Just as you make time for your friends and family, you must equally make time for yourself. Self-care is important for all entrepreneurs because it will help stabilize you mentally, physically, emotionally, and spiritually. We can run ourselves into the ground as business owners as we grind from day to day.

MY SUCCESS AND MY PIVOT

I have been vending for about fifteen years, and I have always had some type of struggle. During the recession, people were not spending money. Online resources give you more access to people you would not have in typical vending scenarios. The pandemic has caused us to do things differently. What will be vending look like after the pandemic? You will need to be online without fail. I have not always had the success in vending I have now. It has been a long journey! I have lost so much over the years in vending but kept on pushing. On some days, I didn't sell at shows. In turn, I would have to go home with all of my products and discount them just to get them out of my house. My successes can be attributed to my ability to

Lessons Learned

pivot. To be a successful entrepreneur, you must be willing to pivot. Many people have been talking about "pivot" during the pandemic like it's a new thing.

I have been pivoting throughout my entire journey as a vendor. I have had to revamp my business over the years based on what I was experiencing. The first change I made was in the area of show selection. I started looking at the types of shows I was vending at. I was tired of wasting money and decided to pick a better quality of shows. During this time, I began to inquire about the shows available.

I networked with people who had been to shows that I had been considering vending at and got their feedback. While I knew their feedback is subjective, I knew some of the information would be helpful in my decision-making process. Networking is also a helpful strategy because you encounter all types of people.

I even paid to attend shows to get the full experience so I would know what I was getting into. I would literally pay for an event as an attendee to get the feel of the show from the attendee position as well as the vendor's position. I knew I was losing money by buying these event tickets, but it was worth it because I needed the information. The information I gathered allowed me to conclude that I didn't need to attend every show and pursue every vending opportunity on the east coast.

After this process, I decided to only participate in quality vending shows. And this was the best decision I could

A Vendor's Guide to Success: How to Go from $0–$100k

have ever made for Jewels by Joan 2. Immediately after deciding to go to only quality events, I started having more success more rapidly. There was a distinct difference between those attending the quality events versus the more low-end shows. Those people attending the quality shows came prepared to shop and spend. They also came to participate in all that the respective shows and events had to offer. They supported the vendors because that was typically the culture of the quality shows.

Although I am not where I desire to be, I am not where I used to be. I also understand that only God allowed me to experience the success I experienced during the pandemic, which is why I decided to write this book. Jewels by Joan 2 grew by leaps and bounds in 2020.

All my shows were getting canceled when the governor was shutting down the state. And all because of one pivot, I went from $0 to $100k during the pandemic just from my Jewels by Joan 2 brand. My 9 to 5 is not part of the 100k—that just became icing on my cake. From the success of Jewels By Joan 2, I was able to fund The Cecilia J Collection debt-free. Did you hear me! Debt Freee! This is a big deal for someone who used to have every credit card known to man and owe everyone in town! So how did I do this? How did I pivot?

The pivot was hosting live shows on social media right from my living room. When I decided to do the Lives, it was from a place of desperation. I wasn't desperate because

106

Lessons Learned

I didn't have a job and income coming in. I was desperate because I didn't know the fate of my vending business. All my shows just started dropping off, and many were not being postponed. They were just being canceled. I'll never forget planning the very first Live.

I only knew I would set up my living room like I was at an actual vending event. I pulled out all my vending supplies and made sure my tablecloth was ready. I then gathered all my devices to go Live on Facebook and Instagram at the same time. Part of me was a little nervous because I didn't know how it would turn out. I asked questions like who will jump on, who will buy, and will I make money? That first Live was quite interesting. My devices had some glitches, and I discovered that trying to go Live on both Facebook and Instagram was too much. After the first Live, I restructured some things and decided it was not feasible to go Live on two platforms. So I decided to go Live on Instagram. I did just Instagram the following week, listened to the feedback from my customers, and saw better results.

Remember I told you that I didn't know how things would work out. By the first week of December of 2020, I had hit the six-figure mark in sales. This was such a major milestone for me, which is why I am writing this book. I have moved past the one-year mark of weekly IG Lives. I have now gone from having one Live a week to having two Lives a week. All of this came as a result of pivoting. Many people assumed that people were not spending

A Vendor's Guide to Success: How to Go from $0–$100k

money during the pandemic, but that was not my experience. My old and new customers supported Jewels by Joan 2 weekly, and my business prospered because of it.

And because of this success, I was able to expand the brand I had launched at the top of 2021. I will be releasing my own line of bags, accessories, and custom garments for The Cecilia J Collection. I am so excited about this launch. I can only expand at this level because of the profit made from my business. You must be clear about how much money you want to make and need to make. While I didn't continue my grandmother's business for money, I do want to make money to grow my business. Investing back into my business is a principle I live by, and I encourage you to do so as well.

Over the years, I have become passionate about helping small business owners. I know it is so competitive out there, and many people say they want to help, but they don't really want to. I wanted to be a beacon of light and hope for those currently in the vending space and those who want to get into the space. I wanted to share my success tips with the world. I see a lot of small business start-ups struggling or stuck. If you are not getting business or sales, it's because you are not consistent, and you are not showcasing yourself. People need to see you and hear you. This is where social media can be your friend. You may be selling shea butter, jewelry, candles, or books—it doesn't matter—you still must be visible. You have to do videos

108

Lessons Learned

and Lives so that people see who you are. If you don't like social media, then you need to partner with someone to bring on your team to help you. Small businesses have struggles that large companies just don't have. Many small businesses don't have a huge budget for things like marketing and branding support. As a small business owner, you are your brand. Let me say that again. When you are small, you are your brand. People need to see various aspects of who you are.

This is key. While I have experienced success over the years, it is not like what I am experiencing now. These qualities, along with the consistent visibility, will prompt people to check out your social media pages, your websites, your Lives, and anything else you do on social media.

Don't hide behind your product if you really plan to win. People must see your face. Some of my coaching clients hide behind their product, and it has stifled their growth.

I had to learn the importance of putting myself out there. When I started, I was a little nervous, but I knew I had to do it. Once I was more active on social media and putting myself out there, I saw my following grow, and as a result, my business grew. Like I said earlier, being in business is a journey, and it is not an overnight success story for many. I have been doing this for fifteen years, and I didn't really start seeing growth until maybe two years ago.

I was successful and was making money here and there, but it was not a consistent flow. Now I have a consistent flow,

A Vendor's Guide to Success: How to Go from $0–$100k

and my business model is much more solid and stable. My overall business brand awareness has intensified, and my profit bottom line has increased. This is hard work, but it is rewarding. This is a journey, and you have to love and want to do this. It must be your passion because your passion will keep you going. Even if you have a 9 to 5 and your business is your side hustle, you must still put in the work. If what you are doing is not your passion, it will eventually fade away.

You won't have a consistent drive and the momentum needed to grow your brand. You may make some coins here and there, but not enough to survive doing it full time. I can't stress enough that you must be in it to win it. If you don't want to win, don't' mess it up for other people. Do what you do, and don't put your mouth on other people in business.

I work hard, and my hard work pays off. I am up late at night while others are sleeping. You will lose some sleep if you want to be successful, but it will be worth it. You will have more work to do than time, but you must get it done.

You have to grind; it is a labor of love. Please know that I wanted to give up many times, and I even took a slight pause from Jewels by Joan 2 because my job was pulling me. But I never gave up but just cut back. Even when I took a pause, I would still set up at a few shows. Listen, don't feel bad if you have to pause your business. Life happens, and most business owners have faced this at some point. What was important to me was being consistent.

Lessons Learned

I remained consistent, which is my keyword. My love for jewelry would not let me stop. I mean, I love jewelry. I love, love, love what I do, and you must love what you do. I love shopping for the things I sell. Bad days can never rob me of loving what I do. If you don't love what you do, it will show. It important for you to stick with your business through thick and thin. If you put it down for a moment, a season, pick it back up. Many people have given up because it is just too much. I don't want that to be your story. While I know everyone is not meant to be an entrepreneur. Some people are called to the workplace and can easily excel at that. I don't believe that is you because you are reading this book. You could use whatever gifts and talents you have to help other entrepreneurs. I want to encourage you to do what is in your heart. If you have a job or resource issues, don't let that stop you from moving your business. You may want everything to be perfect before starting your business, but there will never be a perfect time. Just do it!

So many people come to me and say they want to start a business, but they are scared. I tell them to just do it! Stop and start the business! Launch it! Take it off the ground! Tons of people sell everything you would want to sell and what the consumer will want. The key is to differentiate your brand and market it. You will have competition, but you still can do what God has told you to do. Always sell your competitive advantage and create a

A Vendor's Guide to Success: How to Go from $0–$100k

niche. Turn your fear into faith and faith into favor! You just have to do it! It is in you. You got this!

Love CeCe!

Lessons Learned

Capture any thoughts and comments you have after reading this chapter. How will this chapter help you?

About the Author

Cecilia Penn-Diallo is a native Washingtonian who holds a bachelor's degree in Business Management. With a work-life balance of wife and mom to an AAU student athlete, she earned her MBA from the University of Maryland while working full time. Her motto for multitasking to her success is "faith and family first." Cecilia has been in business for more than ten years and has held various leadership positions throughout a successful career path of over fifteen years. She has become a leading expert on how to start a business in the world of vending and has been called on for advice and wise counsel, especially when it comes to event and project management involving on-site vendors. In 2019, she developed The Vendor Coach, a signature venture that provides mentorship and advice to upstart business owners and event planners. The Vendor Coach was created to help planners, organizers, and new entrepreneurs develop win-win situations for vendor management during their events.

A Vendor's Guide to Success: How to Go from $0–$100k

Her flagship company, Jewels by Joan 2, was born in 2008 out of a legacy of continuation and continues to thrive and grow even through the pandemic of 2020. In her most recent business venture, she designed and created what has become her own line of fashion and accessories, The Cecilia J Collection, which was also launched during the pandemic.

Cecilia continues to promote and encourage business owners to do what she considers one of the most important things they can do for their businesses—*Launch*!

By writing this book, she has given new entrepreneurs and business owners a starting tool to help them realize that they can successfully launch their businesses. She offers tips, advice, and a few hard-earned lessons learned along the way. Cecilia lives in Maryland with her dynamic support team, her husband, Saliou, and their son, Bachir.

Contact

Cecilia J. Penn-Diallo

Facebook: The Vendor Coach

Instagram: @thevendorcoach

Website: www.cecilapenn.com

Booking Information: www.ceciliapenn.com

Email: thevendorcoach@gmail.com

Made in the USA
Middletown, DE
01 August 2021